EX LIBRIS

DOROTHY BEERS

ROSALIND BLISS

MODERN BRITISH
BOOKPLATES

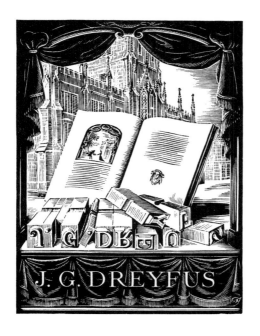

Joan Hassall (1906–88)

BRIAN
NORTH LEE
F·S·A

RICHARD SHIRLEY SMITH

MODERN BRITISH BOOKPLATES

W.E. and D.J. BUTLER

SILENT BOOKS
CAMBRIDGE

First published in Great Britain 1990
by Silent Books, Swavesey, Cambridge CB4 5RA

ISBN 1 85183 023 5

Typeset by Goodfellow and Egan, Cambridge
Printed in Great Britain by St Edmundsbury Press,
Bury St Edmunds, Suffolk

All engravings are reproduced actual size.

Bookplates, or ex libris, are those sticky labels sold by the local stationer. The customer inserts his name in the empty square or line, and pastes them on to the inside cover of his favourite books – or so it is popularly thought. Often the labels are attractively or imaginatively designed and printed, sometimes by designers of distinction. Collectors call such bookplates 'universal ex libris', universal because anyone may purchase them and simply affix their name.

The true bookplate is rather more special – a label specifically designed for the particular library by an artist or printer, or even by the book collector himself where enthusiasm and talent are commensurate. The earliest known marks of ownershp on books originate in ancient Egypt and China; the earliest *printed* ex libris originated in Germany *c.*1450 – fine woodcuts executed by the outstanding practitioners of the period. In England the first bookplate, dated 1574, belonged to Nicholas Bacon, father of the noted jurist-philosopher.

The eighteenth century saw fine copper-engraved armorial bookplates produced in substantial numbers in Britain. Chiefly the work of engravers unknown, they are distinguished by style into categories: Jacobean (*c.*1690–1740), Chippendale (*c.*1740–90) and rococo (*c.*1760–90). Late in the same century wood engraving made its entrance through the inventiveness of Thomas Bewick and his school. Less expensive, capable of producing almost unlimited fine impressions, and well suited to pictorial rather than armorial motifs, wood engraving came to be widely favoured in the nineteenth century, although perhaps the finest work continued to be on copper.

From the 1870s onwards, private collections of ex libris began to be formed on a significant scale and books were produced on the subject. The founding of the Ex Libris Society in London (1891), emulated rapidly by similar societies in Germany, the United States, France, and elsewhere – all with their own illustrated journals – saw an astonishing rise in collecting and an attendant interest in commissioning personal bookplates of a high standard. This was a period of unprecedented collaboration between the owner/patron and the *artist*, as distinct from the tradesman engraver. The finest practitioners on copper, C. W. Sherborn and George W. Eve, were compared to Dürer and his followers. Illustrators produced bookplates no less attractive – Randolph Caldecott, Robert Anning Bell, Henry Ospovat, James Guthrie, E. H. New, Jessie M. King, Kate Greenaway, Arthur Rackham, and dozens of others. Sherborn and Eve alone engraved about 700 bookplates between them.

Bookplate collecting and copper engraving both declined after the First World War for reasons nothing to do with one another. The mantle of bookplate design passed to the wood engravers, who collectively during the 1920s and 1930s and again from the 1970s onwards achieved remarkable standards more than comparable to the Bewick tradition. Illustrators and copper engravers continue to be represented, albeit in relatively small numbers.

URBAN HUTTLESTON
ROGERS
LORD FAIRHAVEN

Stephen Gooden (1892–1955)

THE MODERN ENGLISH BOOKPLATE

The generations past and rising of twentieth-century British wood engravers have been splendidly documented and illustrated by Albert Garrett and Simon Brett (see 'Further Reading'). These are the point of departure for any student of the subject and indeed useful for anyone commissioning a bookplate in order to obtain a wider sense of the artist's style. However, while it is true that the principal developments in British wood engraving are reflected in bookplate design, the converse is not true – bookplate design reveals facets of wood engraving not to be seen in free graphics, book illustration, or commercial engravings.

First, the bookplate is a specially commissioned *personal* design that may combine the owner's profession, interests, library, or any other subject which he desires. Although many bookplates illustrate a particular place or event, symbolic designs are no less popular and challenge the artist's skills of imagination and composition.

Secondly, the bookplate imposes constraints of scale. Mostly they are small, even tiny, engravings – the expression 'miniature graphics' is widely used. As a rule, only artists working in pen and ink enjoy the luxury of reducing large-scale drawings to bookplate size. The others must meet the challenge of working to original scale.

Thirdly, the bookplate combines illustration and text or, especially in Britain where the calligraphic ex libris is esteemed, purely text. Fine lettering is exceptionally demanding, the more so when it must be integrated into and complement pictorial elements. Intimidating any modern practitioner are the examples

Reynolds Stone (1909–79)

of wood-engraved lettering by Reynolds Stone (1909–79) and Leo Wyatt (1909–81), who created more than 360 bookplates or labels each.

Fourthly, bookplates are made to be used in books. Their utilitarian function of designating ownership ought, if properly conceived, to enhance the beauty of book design.

But of course the ultimate test of quality in a bookplate is whether it pleases the owner. For after all, it belongs to him or her and in a certain sense is part of the owner.

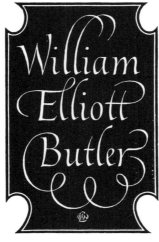

Leo Wyatt (1909–81)

Wood engraving

The wood engravers find it appropriate to classify themselves by generation. All four of this century are active in bookplate design. Pictorial bookplates are within the métier of the great majority, but some engrave calligraphic labels to a very high standard (e.g. Claire Dalby, Michael Renton, Jeffery Matthews) in the tradition of Eric Gill, Stone, and Wyatt. Lettering integrated into the design can be particularly pleasing, although a few engravers may advise that their design be complemented by typeset inscriptions above and/or below the pictorial or armorial element.

English wood engraving has been dominated by what one artist has called the 'haystacks and ferrets' syndrome, eschewing

Zelma Blakeley (1927–78)

social commentary and, on the whole, the human community. Hilary Paynter and Peter Forster are exceptions and may represent a counter-trend. Both approaches are capable of producing exquisite bookplates, and more often than not the designer simply awaits the challenge of creating something novel, something individually special – which the ex libris invariably is.

The range of pictorial choice is virtually unlimited. Leslie Benenson's meticulous engravings of birds and animals, or of figures or scenes from tales and legends, enjoy international patronage. Richard Shirley Smith's exquisitely engraved classical motifs rank among the finest pictorial bookplates of the

14

Douglas Percy Bliss (1900–84)

postwar era. One could continue – but the illustrations tell the full story better than mere words.

Copper engraving

While copper engraving to all appearances flourishes in Britain, those who have designed bookplates are few indeed and of the older generation. The medium is suited to all types of bookplate – pictorial, armorial, and calligraphic – and those who commission heraldic ex libris traditionally have favoured copper. The disadvantage of copper is the relatively small number of fine impressions which can be printed, and this can vary from one artist to another. Modern practitioners include Harry Eccleston, Henry Wilkinson, and Stanley Reece – the latter two having done considerable heraldic work. Perhaps the rising generation of copper engravers merely await patrons.

Drawings

In the two decades before the First World War, Britain's illustrators were enormously influential in bookplate design at home and abroad. Although during the past eight decades

Beresford Egan (1905–84)

individual fine bookplates have been produced in this medium by distinguished practitioners (Beresford Egan, for example), engraving has dominated the field. Illustrators may work either to original scale or produce a large design to be photographically reduced when the plate is made for printing.

Dorothea Braby (1909–87)

Calligraphic labels may be produced in the same way. Will Carter and Ron Smith specialise in lettering for reproduction as book labels, a modestly elegant and popular form of ex libris in Britain.

Typographic labels
Print has a beauty and charm of its own, and it is natural that lovers of fine printing should turn to the printer as a source for marks of ownership which complement the book itself. Effective composition, a pleasing choice of typeface, and perhaps ornamental borders can produce lovely labels. Sebastian and Will Carter and Jonathan Stephenson are among those experienced in typographic ex libris. Sebastian Carter has at his disposal a remarkable set of geometric type elements inherited from the late Hellmuth Weissenborn capable of generating pictorial or representational ex libris designs in the tradition of typographers of the 1920s and 1930s.

COMMISSIONING A BOOKPLATE

COMMISSIONING someone to design a bookplate is simple enough, but careful reflection will be repaid. If you know what you want, it is merely a question of selecting a designer. If you seek information as to what your bookplate might depict, there are several accessible publications (including this one) that may be consulted, especially Severin and Reid, Lee, and Johnson, details of which are given under 'Further Reading'.

Addresses of artists, calligraphers, designers, engravers, and printers who will accept bookplate commissions are given on a separate insert accompanying this volume. It is by no means exhaustive, and you should have no compunction about approaching others or, for that matter, designing one yourself.

The designer you approach will, of course, benefit from all the assistance you can provide by way of ideas or information about yourself and your library. This may include sketches or photographs of specific objects, where appropriate. Designers vary in their work patterns. Most will produce preliminary sketches for your consideration, probably offering two or three basic possibilities and inviting your reaction or approval. Some do a minimum of preliminary artwork and proceed directly to the block or plate.

Price is negotiable in each individual instance and will depend upon the medium chosen, the complexity of the commission, and the distinction of the artist. Prices may range as low as £60 for a linocut or Perspex engraving to as much as £400–500 for a major copper engraving.

It is the usual practice in the United Kingdom for the price quoted to include the cost of preliminary sketches, the original block or plate, and a certain number of artist's signed pulls or

SEBASTIAN CARTER

proofs, all of which become the property of the customer. If in doubt, it is appropriate to inquire. Most designers will (and should be encouraged to) retain pulls or copies of the bookplate for their own professional use (exhibitions, illustration, personal archive, exchange, etc.) or collections. Especially in the case of wood engravings and sometimes copper engravings the artist may stipulate a right to borrow back the block or plate for a reasonable period in connection with an exhibition or special publication; even where not stipulated, it is a normal courtesy to make the block or plate available.

A bookplate design of quality is of little use if badly printed. Consult the designer first about the printing. Some both execute the design and then (at additional cost) print the required number of copies, or arrange the printing with someone who is accustomed to printing their blocks or plates. Advice also should be taken from the designer as to the appropriate shade and texture of paper. You may wish to have 15–25 copies printed on a special handmade paper for framing or gifts.

Britain is blessed with many fine private presses, several of whom have considerable experience in printing wood blocks and copperplates – Will and Sebastian Carter, Simon Lawrence, Michael Mitchell, and Jonathan Stephenson amongst others. Fine white gummed papers are available to facilitate the ex libris being pasted into books.

There are also a number of firms which offer 'universal' bookplates of standard design on which one's name may be printed or written. Major stationers or bookshops are likely to hold stocks of these.

COLLECTING BOOKPLATES

SMALL collections of ex libris are known to have existed in Europe as early as *c*.1717 and in England by the 1820s. Thousands of individuals avidly collect bookplates today and hundreds of libraries and museums hold bookplate collections by bequest or gift. Thirty national societies of bookplate collectors and designers, most of which publish a newsletter, journal, yearbook, and/or books on the subject, have formed an international society known after its French acronym as FISAE (Fédération Internationale des Sociétés d'Amateurs d'Ex-Libris).

The reasons people collect are as many as there are collectors. Some are attracted by the bookplate as a miniature graphic; other specialise in types of design (armorial, pictorial, typographic) or technique (wood engraving, lithograph, photographic), or artist, country, region, or period. Some collect by subject or theme depicted (cats, owls, fish, angels, erotica, printing presses), by owner (families, famous persons, royalty), by geographic area (countries, provinces, counties), by profession (medical, dentistry, legal, authors, architects), or by their own standards of quality or pleasure. Genealogy, iconography, heraldry, bibliography, book studies, printing, and art history all draw upon bookplate collections as sources of data or original works of art. People of all ages and callings collect.

Bookplates may be acquired and a collection started in various ways: bookplates sometimes appear at auction; book dealers, bookbinders, printers, and ephemera specialists occasionally have bookplates for sale individually; artists sometimes present copies of their work, as do librarians examples of their institutional plates. The easiest and most widely practised method,

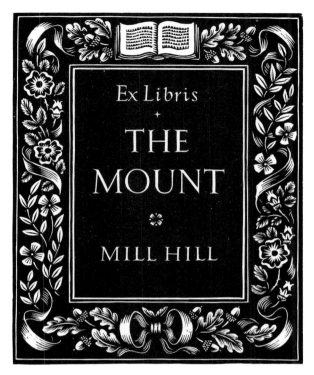

Diana Bloomfield (b. 1915)

though, is to commission your own personal bookplate and reserve a stock for exchange with other collectors.

Joining a bookplate society, or several of them, offers ready access to exchanges and brings the society publications for reference purposes. The first bookplate society in the world was the Ex Libris Society (1891–1908) in London, succeeded in the course of time by The Bookplate Society (1972–), which offers members a fine journal, quarterly newsletter, and a free book annually. In the United States the American Society of Bookplate Collectors and Designers has flourished since 1923; it publishes a quarterly newsletter and a quality yearbook. Mem-

George Mackley (1900–83)

bership of either society is open to all interested persons; addresses are given in the insert accompanying this volume.

To build a collection by exchange it is important to offer quality bookplates by good artists even if some extra expense is involved. The conventions of exchange vary: usually one bookplate for another, but some collectors prefer to exchange one technique for another (e.g. wood engraving for a wood engraving). Rare plates or artists especially esteemed will command a premium. Collectors often commission several different artists to design a bookplate; continental European collectors sometimes have several hundred personal ex libris for exchange. One Italian collector, Mario de Filippis, offers nearly 2,000 on this basis. It requires no mathematical genius to calculate how a collection might grow if a collector has several personal bookplates, each printed in 500 copies, available to exchange.

Although there are certain parallels, collecting ex libris is not like collecting postage stamps. Bookplates are individually commissioned creations; there are no exhaustive definitive catalogues of ex libris, nor can there be. Every collector will make discoveries of previously unknown bookplate designers or ex libris and hopefully contribute his findings to a bookplate society publication. Bookplates are commonly mounted on an appropriate card or paper, lightly affixed with a flour paste at the upper two corners or a double stamp hinge and ordered in boxes by country and artist or, where the artist is unknown, alphabetically by owner. Serious collectors use 'Fincham cases' designed to look and open like a book on the shelf. Corner photo mounts and albums are sometimes used to mount and keep bookplates, although as the collection grows they are not so flexible, even if looseleaf. Archival standard papers and mounts are to be preferred if possible. A bookplate should never be pasted or glued on to a mount in a way that will damage the plate if removed.

The collector should annotate his bookplates carefully. On the back of each ex libris (including those sent for exchange to others) in light pencil should be recorded the name and country of the designer, year in which the plate was designed and printed, and the technique. FISAE has approved a list of standard symbols used by all collectors as a shorthand for designating techniques of ex libris design (reproduced below). Additional annotations are desirable and may, when extensive, be written on the reverse of the bookplate mount: provenance, occupation of the owner, explanation of the design, references to published data on the bookplate or its owner, and any special information about the plate.

Millions of bookplates doubtless exist. No one can say how many may have been created. In bookplate circles a small collection would contain up to 20,000 bookplates, a medium collection up to 50,000, and a large collection in excess of 50,000. The serious collector will in due course acquire the principal reference works on bookplates in addition to joining several bookplate societies.

In the world of bookplate collecting the ex libris acquires

URBAN HUTTLESTON
ROGERS
LORD FAIRHAVEN

Stephen Gooden (1892–1955)

another function or purpose: it becomes a 'passport to friendship'. Exchanging by correspondence augments one's knowledge and can lead to visits or other personal contacts. Most bookplate societies hold meetings at regular intervals where one can become acquainted with fellow collectors, meet designers, acquire plates and literature, and experience the fellowship of collecting. Every two years an international congress under the auspices of FISAE is held for four days, usually in late August, each time in a different country. Belgium, China, the Federal Republic of Germany, Japan, and the Netherlands hold national congresses. Typically a congress features exhibitions of bookplates, perhaps a lecture or two, excursions to local points of interest, and opportunities to meet designers and to exchange personal or duplicate bookplates.

THE DESIGNERS

BARLOW, Naomi (b. 1924). Trained at the Brighton College of Art, she has taught at the Chesterfield, West Sussex and Medway Colleges of Art. Her bookplate designs are pen-and-ink drawings, reduced for reproduction, and she especially enjoys sketching people's homes, adding a decorative border integrating the paraphernalia of their lives.

BATH, Oriol (b. 1939). Taught by Beresford Egan, she works in pen and ink or, occasionally, scraperboard for bookplate designs, having done over 30. The majority of her time is devoted to oil painting, book illustration or, on commission, designing for reproduction on china or porcelain. The latter include remarkable designs after Bilibin and in the art deco tradition.

BEAVEN, Marcus (b. 1944). Wholly self-taught in engraving, he left a furniture-making business in 1973 to pursue his art. He has done book illustrations and published a book of his own wood engravings. Both English and continental collectors have commissioned bookplates from him, and his work has been honoured in international bookplate design competitions. *Ref:* SL.

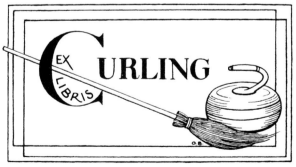

ORIOL BATH

BENENSON, Leslie (b. 1941). Trained as a sculptor at the Regent Street Polytechnic, studying wood engraving with James T. Osborne and calligraphy privately with Anthony Wood. She has designed more than 120 ex libris since 1978 for an international clientele – pictorial and armorial. She has a special flair for animals, especially horses and birds, but her portrayal of mythical figures is equally accomplished. Several bookplate designs have been honoured in international competitions; *Ref: BPJ*, v (1987); *ELEncyc*, ix (1989); *FISAE*, vii (1984); STE; W. E. Butler, *Leslie C. Benenson* (1986).

BLISS, Rosalind (b. 1937). Born in London and educated in Scotland, she is primarily a painter but took up engraving for pleasure in 1971. Although most of her engravings are done for pleasure, she does accept commissions for bookplates. *Ref:* SL; SWE.

BOULTON, Reg. (b. 1924). One of Britain's most productive bookplate designers, he trained in painting, sculpture and pottery at the Bath Academy of Art and Cambridge College of Art. He has pursued wood engraving seriously since 1958, and bookplate design since 1981, on either boxwood or Perspex. Pictorials predominate among

REG BOULTON

his ex libris, but he has done calligraphic and armorial designs. *Ref*: CS; *ELEncyc*, II (1986).

BRETT, Simon (b. 1943). Studied engraving under Clifford Webb at St Martin's School of Art in the early 1960s and then spent some years painting in New Mexico and Provence. Has illustrated several books, some published by his own Paulinus Press, *The Animals of Saint Gregory* having received a coveted Francis Williams Illustration Award. His wood-engraved bookplates number over 80. Brett is the President of the Society of Wood Engravers. *Ref*: B. N. Lee, *The Ex Libris of Simon Brett* (1982); *BPJ*, VII (1989); BWE, CS, *ELEncyc*, IX (1989); HBWE, STE, SWE.

CARTER, Sebastian (b. 1941). A fine designer, printer, and craftsman in partnership with his father, he has designed both typographic and calligraphic book labels and devices. In his possession are the geometrical typographic elements once owned by Hellmuth Weissenborn.

SIMON BRETT

WILL CARTER

CARTER, Will (b. 1912). The eminent Cambridge printer and founder of the Rampant Lions Press, he has designed hundreds of labels, chiefly calligraphic, which he has drawn, reduced, and then reproduced from line blocks with no loss of balance or harmony. The full range of his achievement is best seen in the catalogue to the exhibition at the Fitzwilliam Museum, *The Rampant Lions Press* (1982). *Ref: BPJ*, II (1984).

ANTHONY CHRISTMAS

CHRISTMAS, Anthony (b. 1953). Self-taught as a wood engraver after
training in graphic design. Now resident in Derbyshire, where he
accepts private commissions and operates the Hermit Press, producing private press books with wood-engraved illustrations. *Ref*: CS,
SL, SWE.

CLARKE, Eileen (b. 1941). Trained in printmaking at the NE Essex
School of Art in Colchester, she especially enjoys working in woodcut
and linocut. She prints her bookplate designs on her own Albion
Press, and also has compiled, composed for printing, and illustrated
her own books.

DALBY, Claire (b. 1944). Studied at the City and Guilds School, where
she specialised in lettering. Her bookplates are landscape pictorial,
botanical, and calligraphic. Has engraved in wood since 1967 and
exhibits regularly with the Royal Society of Painter-Etchers and
Engravers, Royal Watercolour Society, Society of Wood Engravers,
and Royal Academy. *Ref*: CS, SWE.

Ex Libris Sue Long

EILEEN CLARKE

ECCLESTON, Harry N. (b. 1923). For a quarter-century the artist designer at the Bank of England Printing Works and sometime President of the Royal Society of Painter-Etchers and Engravers, he has designed pictorial and calligraphic bookplates on both copper and wood. He studied painting until 1942, and taught for many years at the Royal College of Art. The banknotes in your pocket owe much to his skills.

FORSTER, Peter (b. 1934). Learned wood engraving from Mary Maddick and, following an extended sentence as a graphic designer in the Civil Service, went freelance in 1985. Renowned for original and incisive satirical wit and social comment, fully reflected in his

CLAIRE DALBY

HARRY N. ECCLESTON

bookplates, he has done remarkable multi-block colour wood engravings. *Ref*: CS, SL, SWE.

GENTLEMAN, David (b. 1930). One of Britain's outstanding illustrators, he studied under John Nash and Reynolds Stone at the Royal College and credits Thomas Bewick and Eric Ravilious as sources of inspiration. Numerous postage stamps are his work, and millions know his murals at the Charing Cross Underground Station. His bookplates, though not numerous, are in the mainstream of his approach to graphic design. *Ref*: BWE, HBWE, STE, SWE.

JONES, Cordelia (b. 1936). Having discovered engraving through Patricia Jaffé at Cambridge, she illustrated her own book *A Cat Called Camouflage* (1970) and, since 1977, has produced bookplates and ephemera on her own Arab Press. Landscape pictorials and, of course, cats, are a particular strength. *Ref*: *BPJ*, VII (1989); CS, SL, SWE.

JOPE, Anne (b. 1945). Studied at the Central School with Blair Hughes-Stanton and Ian Mortimer. Her pictorial bookplates are imaginative, and in bookplate circles she is believed to have been

PETER FORSTER

the first to depict a computer on an ex libris. *Ref: BPJ*, VII (1989); *ELEncyc*, X (1990) CS, SL, SWE.

KINDERSLEY, David (b. 1915). Apprenticed to Eric Gill for three years, he established his own workshop in 1946 and has become one of the finest exponents of lettering. His bookplates are not engraved, but are drawn and then reproduced, often also reduced. He designed the logo of the XIXth International Ex-Libris Congress at Oxford and has set out his own approach in 'Lettering on bookplates', *BPJ*, I (1983), V (1987).

KING, Simon (b. 1951). A student of Blair Hughes-Stanton and Ian Mortimer, he produces fine book illustrations amongst a variety of creative activities, many for private press editions. *Ref:* CS, STE, SWE.

from
JAMES WILSON'S
books about
FOUNTAINS ABBEY

DAVID GENTLEMAN

Donald & Irene Horwood

CORDELIA JONES

Anne Jope

David Kindersley

SIMON KING

LAWRENCE, John (b. 1933). One of the finest book illustrators in England, he studied engraving with Gertrude Hermes. Some of his best engravings appear in books of his own creation and design, such as *Rabbit and Pork*. He has twice received the Francis Williams Prize for book illustration and is widely known for his colour wash illustrations for *Watership Down*. His fabric art motifs are especially appealing: light-hearted, rich in texture, elaborate in pattern. See P. Guy, 'The wood engravings of John Lawrence', *Matrix*, III (1983), 21–41; BWE, CS, *ELEnyc*, V (1987); *FISAE*, VI (1982); HBWE, STE, SWE.

LEMAIRE, Angela (b. 1944). Born in Buckinghamshire, she studied at the Chelsea and Camberwell schools of art and Morley College, but

JOHN LAWRENCE

KEITH CLARK

ANGELA LEMAIRE

as a wood engraver is self-taught. She has illustrated several privately published books with wood engravings and etchings and is the featured Scottish artist in *FISAE*, VII (1984); *Ref: SL*.

MARTIN, Frank (b. 1921). Freelance illustrator and printmaker, he taught engraving and etching at Camberwell for 27 years. His bookplate designs are principally wood engravings, armorial and

Frank Martin

Jeffery Matthews

RICHARD PARKER

pictorial; they have enriched English bookplate design for more than four decades. *Ref*: BWE, CS, HBWE, STE, SWE.

MATTHEWS, Jeffery (b. 1928). London-born in a family of distinguished goldsmiths, he has worked freelance since 1952. Early training included heraldry and calligraphy. An eminent postage stamp designer, he took up wood engraving in 1974 and has designed several bookplates which he prints from the block on an antique Albion Press. *Ref*: SL.

PARKER, Richard (b. 1953). Dividing his time between painting and engraving, he has done pictorial and armorial bookplate designs. His skills in heraldic devices are illustrated in a planned private press book containing over forty engravings of the armorials of all the Oxford colleges and private halls. *Ref*: *ELEncyc*, XI (1990) SL. Recent work appears under the name of Richard Parker Crook.

HILARY PAYNTER

PAYNTER, Hilary (b. 1943). One of the bundles of energy behind the
revival of the Society of Wood Engravers, she spent much of her early
life abroad, in China and Malta, and studied engraving with Gerry
Tucker at Portsmouth. Her bookplates are reflective of her wide
range in choice of subjects, from social commentary to the fate of
mankind. Her wood-engraved illustrations for private press books
include work for the Gryphon Press, the Whittington Press and a
view of George Orwell's Hampstead bookshop for a Dutch press. *Ref:*
BPJ, VI (1988); BWE, CS, *ELEncyc*, VI (1988); HBWE, STE, SWE.

PAYNTON, Colin (b. 1946). Excelling in intricately patterned scenes of
wild life, he lives in Wales and is self-taught as a wood engraver. Has

39

COLIN PAYNTON

illustrated books for several private presses and succeeds in tran-
scending the canons for depicting natural life in a remarkable way.
Ref: CS. SWE.

POOLE, Monica (b. 1921). A student of John Farleigh at the Central
School, her wood engravings are exquisitely crafted – often botanical
themes – sometimes stark, other times gentle. Her bookplates are

MONICA POOLE

few, but very much in the mainstream of her approach. *Ref:* G. Mackley (intro), *Monica Poole – Wood Engraver* (1984); BWE, CS, HBWE, STE, SWE.

RAWLINSON, William T. (b. 1912). Born in Liverpool, he studied at the College of Art in that city and then on the continent. Painter, teacher, and wood-engraver, characterised by Albert Garrett as 'The English master of the overall half-tone optical grey of engraving', untouched by the dominating influences and aesthetic theories of his day in England, an independent free agent, his pictorial bookplates are principally landscape. *Ref:* BWE, CS, HBWE, STE, SWE.

REDDICK, Peter (b. 1924). Noted as a book illustrator, principally wood engravings, he also does watercolours and colour woodcuts. His bookplates are mostly landscape pictorials. *Ref:* BWE, CS, HBWE, STE, SWE.

WILLIAM T. RAWLINSON

REECE, Stanley (b. 1932). A copper engraver who trained with G. T. Friend, he has designed numerous armorial bookplates, and lectures part-time on engraving at the Sir John Ross School of Arts in London and the Royal College of Art. He is a Freeman of the Worshipful Company of Goldsmiths and a member of the Society of Designer Craftsmen. *Ref: BPJ*, VIII (1990).

RENTON, Michael (b. 1934). Apprenticed in London to one of the last firms of commercial wood-engravers, he has worked freelance since 1960. His interests include decorative panels on wood and stone, paintings of rural scenes, designing articles for everyday use, letter-heads, and the like. His bookplates are principally allegorical, calligraphic, or pictorial; he is author of the introduction to *The*

PETER REDDICK

Engraved Bookplates of Eric Gill (1987). *Ref:* CS, *ELEncyc*, VII (1988); *FISAE*, V (1980); STE, SWE.

RILEY, Derek (b. 1931). Sculptor, wood-engraver, private pressman, and bibliophile, he is amongst the most prolific of English ex libris designers – pictorial and calligraphic, often with a Celtic bent. A bookplate collector too, he welcomes exchanges. *Ref: ELEncyc*, I (1985).

SCULLARD, Sue (b. 1958). Pupil of Yvonne Skargon at the Royal College, she is a freelance illustrator with numerous book illustrations to her credit. Landscape, especially hills and mountains, and decorative subjects are a speciality. Engraves on wood, lino, and vinyl. *Ref:* CS, SWE.

SMITH, Peter (b. 1946). Painter and printmaker, and Head of Art and Design at the Kingston College of Further Education, he has turned only recently to wood engraving, where his work is full of mood, restrained, and founded on personal experience. *Ref:* CS, SWE.

SMITH, Richard Shirley (b. 1935). Self-taught in wood engraving, he is amongst the finest practitioners of the art, achieving superlative levels

AMOR SCALA CŒLO

Ex Libris
GEOFFREY RALPH EVANS

STANLEY REECE

44

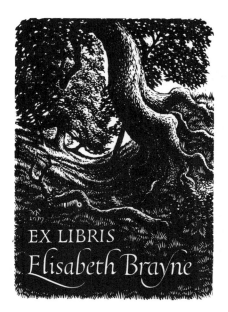

MICHAEL RENTON

of perfection and exquisiteness of line. Bookplates are a major aspect of his oeuvre, but he also works in collage and murals. Educated at the Slade School, University College London, he studied under Anthony Gross and is much influenced by David Jones. Often his ex libris combine portraiture with classical motifs. *Ref: BPJ*, III (1985); BWE, CS, *ELEncyc* IV (1986); HBWE, STE, SWE.

SMITH, Ron (b. 1932). Studied lettering and design at the City and Guilds of London Art School; and specialises in calligraphic and typographic labels. Inspired by Reynolds Stone, he found the pen better suited to his style and has set up as a freelance designer. His labels have been awarded prizes on the continent.

STEPHENS, Ian (b. 1940). Having pursued engraving part-time since 1961 and become a full-time freelance in 1990, his work emphasises the place of man in the natural world in the eyes of the artist. His bookplate designs are principally pictorial, although calligraphic plates are well within his range. *Ref*: CS, SL, SWE.

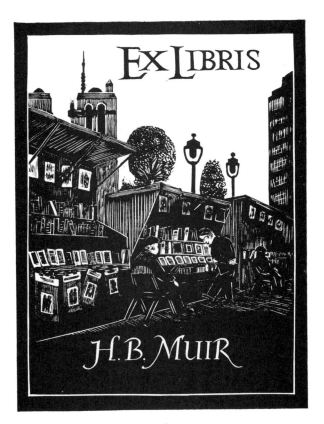

EX LIBRIS

H. B. MUIR

DEREK RILEY

STEPHENSON, Jonathan (b. 1964). A boy prodigy as a printer, he has already made his mark as one of the fine private pressmen through his Rocket Press. Typographic labels always have had a special charm since the seventeenth century. He has a considerable range of ornamental devices and founts and is happy to design to order.

VAN NIEKERK, Sarah (b. 1934). Studied with Gertrude Hermes at the Central School and with Lynton Lamb and Anthony Gross at the Slade School, University College London. She produces primarily

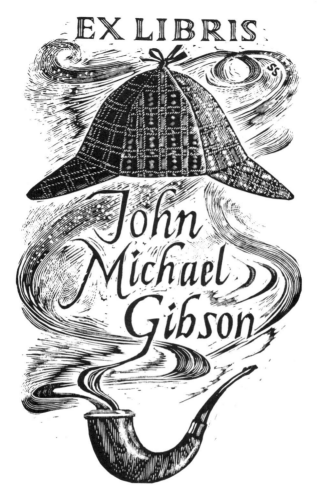

EX LIBRIS

John
Michael
Gibson

SUE SCULLARD

free graphics and book illustrations and also does linocuts. Her
wood-engraved bookplates favour landscapes and animals as subjects.
Ref: BPJ, VI (1988); BWE, CS, HBWE, STE, SWE.

WILKINSON, Henry (b. 1912). An all-round artist-craftsman, his work includes medals, sporting prints, gold and silverware, stone masonry, metal plaques, guns, cabinets, and copper-engraved bookplates. For years he was Professor of the Engraving School of the City and Guilds of London. Has done hundreds of bookplates, though in recent years he has concentrated on oil paintings and engravings of sporting gun dogs. *Ref: BPJ*, IV (1986).

WILLIAMS, Ray (b. 1931). Educated at the Epsom School of Art, he became a photographer for *Vogue* and teaches at the Bath Academy of Art. He does some printing and screen printing; his bookplates are line drawings printed lithographically. His preference is designing pictorial bookplates depicting a single theme or story.

RON SMITH

WORMELL, Christopher (b. 1955). After years as a painter, took up wood engraving in 1982 and has produced hundreds of commercial wood engravings for *The Times* and dozens of publishers. His bookplate for Michael Mooney graced the poster of the first exhibition of modern British bookplates in the Soviet Union. *Ref*: CS, SWE.

FURTHER READING

I F you seek inspiration as to what your bookplate design might contain, there are several publications worth consulting: M. Severin and A. Reid, *Engraved Bookplates: European Ex Libris 1950–70* (Pinner, Private Libraries Association, 1972) contains a chapter on commissioning a bookplate (pp. 13–18) and offers sound advice to would-be collectors. F. Johnson, *A Treasury of Bookplates from the Renaissance to the Present* (New York, Dover, 1977) is lightweight in text but illustrates examples from all over the world. Learned and profusely illustrated is Brian North Lee, *British Bookplates: A Pictorial History* (London, David and Charles, 1979). The standard work on American bookplates is W. E. and D. J. Butler, *The Golden Era of American Bookplate Design: 1890–1940* (Frederikshavn, K. Rodel, 1986).

Your local bookshop may have other titles. Do not be put off if your bookshop says not many books are published on the subject – the largest European collections of books on bookplates contain in excess of 5,000 titles.

For sixteen years a Portuguese collector published substantial volumes with tipped-in plates containing biographies of artists around the world. Seven volumes appeared in all between 1968 and 1984 inclusive, and each is a collector's item. The series was superseded in 1986 by the *Encyclopedia Bio-Bibliographical of the Art of the Contemporary Ex-Libris* edited by A. da Mota Miranda. The artists' biographies are accompanied by checklists of their bookplates. Twelve volumes had been published by 1990 in this continuing series.

See the list of abbreviations for references to other works reproducing a broader range of wood engravings by artists mentioned here. Of particular importance is S. Brett (comp. & intro.), *Engravers: A Handbook for the Nineties* (Cambridge, Silent Books, 1987), in soft cover.

IAN STEPHENS

ABBREVIATIONS

BPJ   *The Bookplate Journal*, published twice yearly by The Bookplate Society since 1983.

BWE   A. Garrett, *British Wood Engraving of the Twentieth Century* (London, Scolar, 1980).

CS   *A Cross Section: The Society of Wood Engravers in 1988* (Wakefield, Fleece Press, 1988).

ELEncyc   *Encyclopaedia Bio-Bibliographical of the Art of the Contemporary Ex-Libris*, ed. A. M. da Mota Miranda (Celorico de Basto, Miranda, 1986–).

FISAE   Fédération Internationale des Sociétés d'Amateurs d'Ex-Libris. *Ex Libris Artists*, ed. A. M. da Mota Miranda (Lisbon, A.P.E.L., 1968–84). 7 vols.

HBWE   A. Garrett, *A History of British Wood Engraving* (Tunbridge Wells, Midas, 1978).

SL   *45 Wood Engravers*, intro. by John Lawrence (Wakefield, Simon Lawrence, 1982).

STE   *S. T. E. Lawrence, Boxwood Blockmaker* (Wakefield, Simon Lawrence, 1980).

SWE   S. Brett (comp. & intro.), *Engravers: A Handbook for the Nineties* (Cambridge, Silent Books, 1987).

Leo John De Freitas

JONATHAN STEPHENSON

John Piper (b. 1903)

TECHNICAL SYMBOLS FOR BOOKPLATES

As approved in 1958, with subsequent amendments, by the International Ex-Libris Congress at Barcelona.

B   Braille

C   Intaglio printing
C1   Steel engraving
C2   Copper engraving

SARAH VAN NIEKERK

54

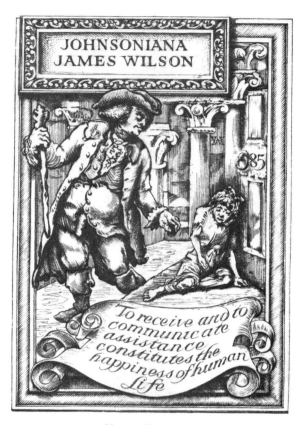

HENRY WILKINSON

C3 Etching
C4 Drypoint
C5 Aquatint
C6 Soft-ground etching
C7 Mezzotint

NICHOLAS
LANGMAN

Ray Williams

56

X	Relief printing
X1	Woodcut
X2	Wood engraving
X3	Lino cut
X4	Lead engraving
X5	Zinc engraving
X6	Plastic engraving

L	Lithography

S	Silk screen

P	Photographic reproduction
P1	Line block
P2	Half-tone
P3	Photogravure
P4	Rotagravure
P5	Collotype
P6	Photolithography
P7	Offset
P8	Photograph

T	Typographic

E	Calligraphy

When bookplates are produced in more than one colour, the symbol should be followed by a vertical stroke and the number of colours used; e.g. X2/3 means a wood engraving printed from the block in three colours, whereas X2/col. indicates a wood engraving with hand-colouring.

CHRISTOPHER WORMELL

EX LIBRIS

Malcolm Muggeridge

NAOMI BARLOW